First published in 2025 by Welbeck Children's Books
An imprint of Hachette Children's Group
Copyright © 2025 Hodder & Stoughton Limited
Author: Desma Palmer-Fettig

The publishers would like to thank the following sources for their kind
permission to reproduce the pictures in this book.

SHUTTERSTOCK (used throughout the book): A_Nordia; Alina Pear; Cadmi-
um_Red; Christos Georghiou; Collaborapix Studio; Dariagalitsyna; Dergriza;
Dergriza; Genggggg; Kaleb-Silva; Ksuper; La Gorda; Mitrnight; N.Ptashka;
NastyaTsy; Nurin Nabila A; Perfect_Vectors; Rahmat DJayusman; Roberto Ma-
rantan; Takoyaki Tech; Tartila; Vector Tradition; VectorPixelStar; Wernerwitch.

A CIP catalogue record for this book is available from the British Library.

ISBN 978 1 80453 815 9
Printed in the UK
10 9 8 7 6 5 4 3 2 1

Welbeck Children's Books
An imprint of Hachette Children's Group
Part of Hodder & Stoughton Limited
Carmelite House, 50 Victoria Embankment
London EC4Y 0DZ

The authorised representative in the EEA is Hachette Ireland,
8 Castlecourt Centre, Dublin 15, D15 XTP3, Ireland (email: info@hbgi.ie)

An Hachette UK Company
www.hachette.co.uk
www.hachettechildrens.co.uk

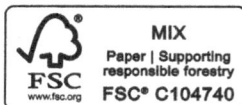

MIX
Paper | Supporting
responsible forestry
FSC® C104740
FSC
www.fsc.org

CHOOSE IT!
VIDEOGAME EDITION

Desma Palmer-Fettig

WELBECK
CHILDREN'S BOOKS

Game on! Would you rather be able to...?

☐ Shoot magical light arrows to banish evil like Princess Zelda

OR

Breath fire at your enemies like Charizard ☐

☐ Jump up high like Super Mario

OR

Run fast like Sonic the Hedgehog ☐

HERO POWERS

How about building powers...?

☐ Build with different blocks like Steve and Alex from *Minecraft*

OR

Build huge towers in seconds like in *Fortnite* ☐

What's the source of your powers...?

☐ Copy powers from the things you eat like Kirby

OR

Get power-ups from your clothing like Link ☐

BIG BAD BOSSES

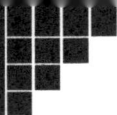

Videogame bosses are always a challenge,
but would you rather fight...?

☐ The Ender Dragon without ANY armour **OR** Dr. Eggman without ANY rings ☐

Oh no! Now the Bosses are teaming up!
Will you take on...?

☐ Meta-Knight AND King Boo at the same time **OR** Wario AND Bowser at the same time ☐

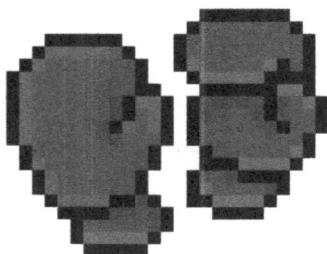

BOSS STAGES

Which boss lair mix-up would you rather face?

☐ Ganon in the Nether

OR

The Ender Dragon in Bowser's Castle ☐

Not all boss showdowns need to be a fight! How about challenging...?

☐ Meta-Knight to a game of basketball

OR

Dr. Eggman to a game of chess ☐

SPEED BOOST

Uh-oh! You're late for school! How do you get there in time?

☐ Hitch a ride on Kirby's Warp Star   **OR**   Get Sonic to give you a piggyback ride ☐

Link is helping you with his Ultra Hand powers. What will you make?

☐ Ten rockets stuck together   **OR**   A Moblin-powered monster truck ☐

You've been challenged to a race on Rainbow Road!

☐ Place banana peels the night before to slow the other racers down

OR

Practise every day for a whole week before the race ☐

Your school bus broke down. Who's taking you to school?

☐ Bowser in a spiky, fire-breathing airship

OR

The legendary Pokémon, Miraidon, heeds your call ☐

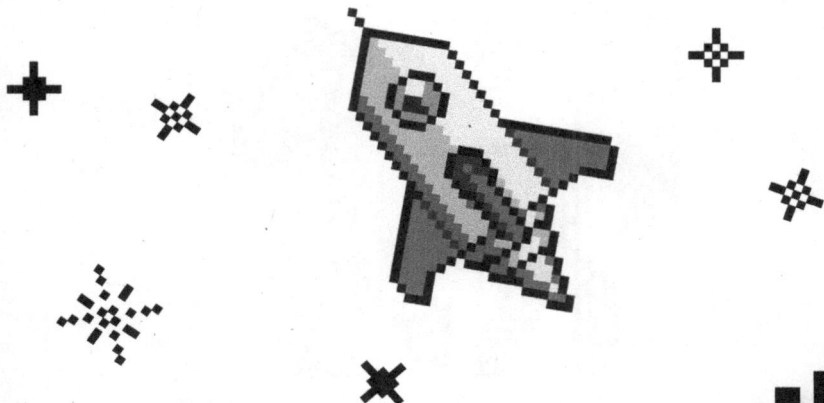

GIDDY UP

Helping out at the Pokémon stables, what's the toughest part of the job?

☐ Getting covered in dirt by Mudsdale

OR

Stopping Rapidash from setting the stable on fire ☐

Princess Zelda is waiting for you at Hyrule Castle! Ride there...?

☐ On the back of Satori, the Lord of the Mountain

OR

On a skeletal Stalhorse beneath the pale moonlight ☐

Which item would you rather get in *Mario Kart*...?

☐ Infinite Green Shells you can throw every three seconds?

OR

One Blue Shell at the beginning of every lap? ☐

What about adding an item from a different game? Would you rather use...?

☐ The Booyah Bomb from *Splatoon* to explode around you?

OR

A Creeper from *Minecraft* to chase racers behind you? ☐

HEROES & VILLAINS

Heroes and villains are teaming up to help you out! Who will you pick?

☐ Luigi and Shadow the Hedgehog

OR

☐ Big Man and DJ Octavio

OR

☐ Peely and Flowey

OR

☐ Princess Rosalina and GLaDOS

HEROES & VILLAINS

Who would you rather have on your side...?

☐ Sonic without sneakers and Dr. Eggman without robots

OR

☐ A Donkey Kong-sized Pikmin and a Pikmin-sized Donkey Kong

OR

☐ Captain Toad and an Enderman

OR

☐ A stack of Goombas and Jonesy with just a pickaxe

♡ ♡ ♡ ♡ ♥ ♥ ♥

13

HEROES & VILLAINS

What about a team up between...?

☐ Kirby and King Dedede

OR

Champion Nemona and Team Rocket ☐

Which fuzzy hero and mad scientist combo would you rather help?

☐ Tawna Bandicoot and Neo Cortex

OR

Ratchet and Dr. Nefarious ☐

FANTASTIC FACTS

Minecraft is the single best-selling video game in the world. It has sold over 350,000,000 copies. That's a lot of blocks!

Yoshis prefer different fruits depending on what colour the Yoshi is! However, they *all* love melons.

REST & RELAXATION

At which *Mario Kart* course would you rather spend your holiday?

☐ Merry Mountain in the wintertime

OR

Dolphin Shoals in the summertime ☐

An island getaway! Would you rather visit...?

☐ A perfect *Animal Crossing* island, but you'll owe Tom Nook 1 million Bells

OR

Cheep Cheep Beach, but your hotel is right next to the race track ☐

SUMMERTIME FUN

How do you pass the time on holiday?

☐ Swim with a pod of Finizen (dolphin Pokémon) at the Pokémon Resort

OR

Flying on a Loftwing around Hyrule ☐

How would you rather spend your summer?

☐ Going to summer camp in the world of *Splatoon*

OR

Helping out at a Pokémon Daycare ☐

KEEPING COOL

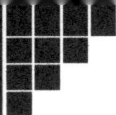

You're exploring Death Mountain's volcano, how do you stay cool?

☐ Craft Fireproof Elixirs to protect you

OR

Wear the uncomfortable Firebreaker armour ☐

There's a lava pool blocking the way! How do you cross?

☐ Borrow Kirby's ice powers and skate over top

OR

Use a Blastoise to cool the lava so you can walk across ☐

You're climbing a frozen mountain, how will you stay warm?

☐ Bring a fire-type Pokémon to protect you from the cold

OR

Wear a Snowquill suit from Rito Village ☐

An avalanche is heading your way! What do you do?

☐ Use a Fire Rod to cast heat magic and melt it

OR

Ride your shield like a snowboard and enjoy it ☐

HAUNTED MANSION

**You're going to bust ghosts with Luigi!
Would you rather...?**

☐ Use the dark-light to find hidden secrets

OR

Use the vacuum to suck up ghosts ☐

Would you rather help Luigi explore...?

☐ A haunted theme park with clown ghosts

OR

A haunted Wild West town with cowboy ghosts ☐

Which ghost would you rather be followed by for a day?

☐ A Boo that keeps sneaking behind you when you're not looking

OR

A Gengar that hangs out in your shadow and blows raspberries at everyone ☐

Would you rather have a Boo House be...

☐ Right across from school

OR

Down the street from your house ☐

WHEELY GOOD

Which video game power-up would you add to a real car?

☐ A rocket and a Turbo Mode button

OR

A Jump button and a glider from *Mario Kart* ☐

Which hero-car combo would you rather drive?

☐ Car Mouth Kirby that eats snacks for fuel

OR

A Pac-Man shaped car that eats dots for fuel ☐

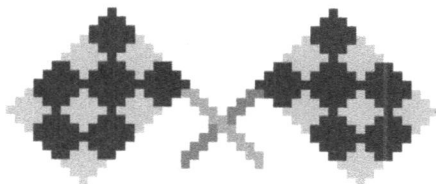

Which would you rather do?

Ride through the clouds on a Tallneck from *LEGO Horizon Adventures*

OR

Go on an undersea journey with Clanker from *Banjo-Kazooie*

Which robot will you control?

A Redstone Golem that you have to build yourself

OR

A giant ROB the Robot that you control with an old game pad

Would you rather ride around with your friends in...?

☐ A Flying Pikachu Blimp **OR** The Battle Bus from *Fortnite* ☐

Which flying machine would you rather take to school?

☐ Ride on top of Tails' plane - the Tornado **OR** Drive a fan-powered hoverbike from *Tears of the Kingdom* ☐

While crossing the sea, would you rather...?

☐ Take it easy on the Daisy Cruiser from *Mario Kart*

OR

Dip your toes while on the back of a Lapras? ☐

What if you had to travel under the water? Would you rather take...?

☐ A fast submarine disguised as a giant Blooper from *Super Mario*

OR

The advanced NEO-ONE research vehicle from *New Pokémon Snap* ☐

DREAM JOB

Would you rather work...?

☐ At Nintendo BUT you have to always talk like the Mario Bros

OR

Making **Roblox** games, BUT you look like a default avatar in real life ☐

What if you worked inside of a game? Would you rather...?

☐ Run a restaurant for King Dedede and cook all his meals

OR

Work at a Pokémon Center at the top of Mt. Coronet ☐

Why did the Toads invite Mario to their party?

BECAUSE HE'S A FUN GUY.

JUST JOKING!

Why did the skeleton run away from Link?

IT DIDN'T HAVE THE GUTS TO FIGHT HIM.

Would you rather have to play...?

☐ *Splatoon* with your family on your team

OR

Fortnite with your teacher on your team ☐

How about a cooking contest? First one to...?

☐ Bake a cake in *Minecraft*, outdoors, at night, with no torches

OR

Make a pizza in the middle of a Big Yeetus hammer arena ☐

**It's an all-you-can-eat challenge!
Would you rather...?**

☐ Inhale all the food at once as Kirby **OR** Slurp each thing up with a Yoshi tongue ☐

The courses in *Fall Guys* are already tough, but let's make them even tougher!

☐ Race King Dedede in an eating contest through Fall Mountain **OR** Collect the most Sonic rings through Hex-A-Gone ☐

SUIT UP!

When it comes to armour, *Minecraft* has you covered! But would you rather...?

☐ Wear totally random armour pieces every single in-game day

OR

Have one armour set that never breaks but is your least favourite colour ☐

Would you rather get to play as...?

☐ Luigi wearing an old knight's suit of armour

OR

Rouge the Bat wearing futuristic armour ☐

ENCHANTED ARMOUR

Would you rather be able to enchant
all your clothes with...?

Magic pockets
that can hold
hundreds of
objects

OR

Magic thread
that means you
never get too
hot or too cold,
no matter the
weather

Would you rather enchant a shirt so that
whenever you wear it, you...?

Never get tired,
but you're stuck
looking like
Minecraft Steve

OR

Look like a new
Fortnite skin
every day, but
you can't control
which one

Which *Super Mario* hat would you rather own in real life?

☐ A Wing Cap that lets you fly, but it's tricky to control

OR

A Metal Cap that makes you tough but heavy ☐

Which hat would you rather have to wear to school for a month?

☐ The Eerie Pumpkin Head from ***Roblox***

OR

A Creeper Head from ***Minecraft*** ☐

SHIELDS READY

Would you rather have a shield that

□ ...protects you from any attack, but it's so heavy you can't move when using it

OR

...reflects anything back, but runs out of energy quickly □

If you could add shields to a game that doesn't have them, which would you pick...?

□ *Mario Kart*, but the shield only works when you close your eyes

OR

Splatoon, but the shield only works if you're dancing in real life □

IF THE SHOE FITS

Which pair of famous gaming shoes would you rather wear every day for a year?

☐ Sonic's classic sneakers?　**OR**　Mario's classic boots? ☐

Which shoe power would you pick?

☐ The Pegasus Boots from *Legend of Zelda* so you can dash everywhere　**OR**　Chell's Long Fall Boots from *Portal*, so you never get hurt if you take a tumble ☐

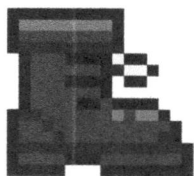

DISGUISES

A scary squad of monsters is headed your way! What do you do?

☐ Try to make friends by inviting them to your *Animal Crossing* town for a picnic

OR

Use one of Link's monster masks to blend in ☐

There's a school disco next week! What do you wear?

☐ Borrow clothes from your favourite *Fortnite* character

OR

Wear your character's clothes from *Stardew Valley* ☐

CLEVER COMPANIONS

When studying for a spelling test, would you rather get help from...?

☐ Tails the twin-tailed Fox

OR

Beep-0 the floating supercomputer from *Mario + Rabbids* ☐

Uh oh, your games console is on the fritz. Who do you ask to help fix it?

☐ Coco the computer whiz from *Crash Bandicoot*

OR

Penny the hacker from *Pokémon Scarlet and Violet* ☐

Which villain mashup would make a better sidekick?

☐ Dr. Eggman with Bowser's strength and powers

OR

Bowser with one of Dr. Eggman's boss machines ☐

Which hero mashup would you rather team up with?

☐ Knuckles, but he's as tall as a bus

OR

THREE Donkey Kongs... but they're all the size of a cat ☐

Who would you rather have on your football team?

☐ Knuckles and Amy, but the rest of the team are Chao

OR

Luigi and Princess Peach, but the rest of the team are Goombas ☐

Who would you rather have on your rounders team?

☐ Donkey Kong and Rouge, but the rest of your team are Shy Guys

OR

Bowser and Daisy, but the rest of your team are Waddle Dees ☐

FANTASTIC FACTS

The biggest Pokémon is Eternatus, the Poison/Dragon type, at a gigantic 20 metres long!

There are at least 8 Pokémon tied as the smallest, including Joltik, Flabébé and Cutiefly, measuring just 10 centimetres long!

HOME SWEET HOME

Would you rather live in a house of *Minecraft* blocks made of...?

☐ Wool, so nothing makes a sound

OR

Deepslate, with no windows and only torches for light ☐

Would you rather have a bathroom that...?

☐ Plays the *Super Mario* theme whenever you flush the toilet

OR

Is haunted by a Boo which you can only see in the mirror ☐

HOME SWEET HOME

Who would you rather have to live with...?

The Koopalings and Bowser Jr. in a castle surrounded by lava

OR

The Kong family in a treehouse on a jungle island

Which *Mario Kart* track would you rather call home?

Sky-High Sundae, with huge ice cream buildings floating in the sky

OR

Sweet Sweet Canyon, a place made from giant treats and sweets

FRUIT FESTIVAL

Which fruit smoothie would you drink?

☐ Sitrus Berry smoothie from *Pokémon*

OR

Wumpa Fruit smoothie from *Crash Bandicoot* ☐

Which *Super Mario* fruit power would you want to try?

☐ The Double Cherry to make a copy of yourself

OR

The Elephant Fruit to transform you into a powerful elephant ☐

Which vegetable dish would you rather have on your plate?

☐ Roasted Cave Roots from *Stardew Valley*   **OR**   A *Minecraft* pumpkin block ☐

Which vegetable makes for a better weapon?

☐ Captain Toad's Turnip Cannons   **OR**   Sirfetch'd Leek Lance ☐

POTION POWERS

Which two *Minecraft* potions would you rather have in real life?

☐ Potion of Water Breathing AND Potion of Swiftness

OR

Potion of Invisibility AND Potion of Night Vision ☐

Enemy NPCs are on your tail! Which *Terraria* potion will you drink to help escape?

☐ Featherfall Potion so you can jump to safety

OR

Builder Potion so you can quickly build a safe fort ☐

Why is Sonic banned
from the park?

**BECAUSE HE'S
A HEDGE HOG!**

JUST JOKING!

Why did Mario cross
the road?

**TO GET TO THE
NEXT LEVEL!**

PICK A SIDE QUEST

Which side quest would you rather take during break time?

☐ A quest to collect all of the teacher's missing pencils

OR

A quest to help a lost cat sneak through the playground without being seen ☐

Which side quest would you pick on the way home from school?

☐ Collecting ten secret coins hidden around the neighbourhood

OR

Protecting a neighbour from a horde of *Minecraft* Zombies ☐

A friend needs protection from some mean bullies. Do you...?

Bring them a Super Mushroom to make them big and scary

OR

Build a redstone trap to stop the bullies in their tracks

You need to sneak into school after the lights are out to find a lost item! Are you going to...?

Bring a glowing yellow Yoshi to grab the item with its tongue

OR

Copy Sheik's ninja style and try to stay hidden

MUSICAL MELODIES

If you had an Ocarina of Time, which song would you rather learn?

Song of Healing, to help make anyone feel better

OR

Song of Double Time, to make the day go by faster

Besides an Ocarina, what instrument would you rather play to make magic happen?

Donkey Kong's bongo drums

OR

KK Slider's guitar

If you were a video game boss, what would your boss music sound like?

☐ Roaring rock music with electric guitar

OR

Epic classical music with piano and violin ☐

Which would you rather have to listen to all day?

☐ A room full of Gyroids from *Animal Crossing*

OR

Banjo and Kazooie playing... a banjo and a kazoo! ☐

STRANGE SOUVENIRS

While travelling the *Mario Odyssey* kingdoms, would you rather take home...

☐ A spacey snowglobe from the Moon Kingdom

OR

One collectable postcard from each kingdom ☐

Which silly hat would you rather get as a souvenir?

☐ A hat with Pikachu ears that lets you zap anyone who shakes your hand

OR

A hat shaped like a *Minecraft* Villager that plays their sound effects whenever you enter a room ☐

Which t-shirt would you rather be stuck wearing?

'Welcome to the Fungle' from *Among Us*  A default *Roblox* avatar with a speech bubble saying 'OOF!'

Who would you rather take vacation selfies with?

Meowscles  Rabbid Peach

ROWDY ROOMATES

Which roommates would you rather live with?

☐ Bowser Jr who turns his half of your room into a boss lair

OR

Timmy and Tommy from *Animal Crossing* who set up a shop ☐

Who would you rather share a wall with...?

☐ A cave full of Creepers from *Minecraft*

OR

A meeting room from *Among Us* that sounds a siren for every meeting called ☐

FANTASTIC FACTS

Dr. Eggman was always called 'Eggman' in Japan from the start. But he was called 'Robotnik' in other parts of the world, until years later when it was decided to call him 'Eggman' everywhere.

Princess Peach used to be called 'Princess Toadstool' in many parts of the world. 'Toadstool' is a type of mushroom. But she was always called 'Peach' in Japan.

HAIRY HARDWARE

Would you rather have a game controller that is made of...?

☐ Goopy purple slime **OR** Fuzzy green fur ☐

Would you rather have a game console that...?

☐ Is also an adorable animal, but needs to eat 10 bananas every day to work **OR** Is wired through your house so you can play in every room, but always knows when your homework is due ☐

Would you rather have...?

☐ A controller that can read your thoughts so you don't need to press buttons to play

OR

A screen that makes your game look like homework to everyone else ☐

Would you rather have a game system that is...?

☐ Pedal-powered and works even when the power's out

OR

Super powerful but solar-powered, so can only be played during the day ☐

Would you rather have the world record for...?

☐ Speedrunning a **Super Mario** game while riding a hot air balloon

OR

Speedrunning a **Sonic** game while riding a rollercoaster ☐

Would you rather have the world record for...?

☐ The biggest collection of Froggy Chairs in **Animal Crossing**

OR

The biggest collection of Magikarp in **Pokémon** ☐

Would you rather have the world record for...?

Shouting the loudest "Wahoo" in a Mario voice

OR

Building the tallest tower made only of dirt blocks in *Minecraft*

Would you rather have the world record for...?

Falling off *Fall Guys* stages the most times

OR

Getting ejected from *Among Us* the most times

PLACES TO PLAY

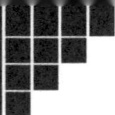

Which would you rather have for long car rides?

☐ A fancy gaming setup to play any game ever

OR

A way to video chat with characters from any one game ☐

Would you rather play *Mario Kart*...?

☐ While riding an eel underwater

OR

While riding a minecart in a volcano ☐

Would you rather have to play *Fall Guys*...?

☐ While sledding down a mountain **OR** While biking through a desert ☐

Would you rather have to play *Stardew Valley*...?

☐ While bungee jumping off a bridge **OR** While skydiving ☐

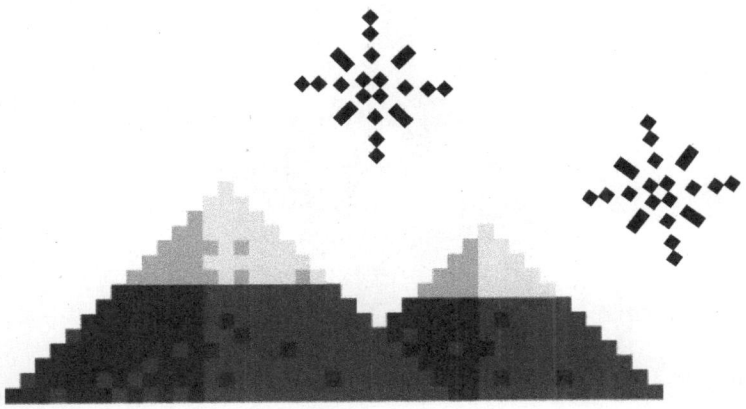

PLACES TO PLAY

Would you rather have to play *Among Us*...?

☐ In a creepy, cobweb-filled attic

OR

At school at night in the dark ☐

Would you rather play *Minecraft*...

☐ In the woods next to a campfire

OR

Out on a boat on a lake ☐

Why did Luigi bring an extra pair of pants to the Mushroom Kingdom's golf tournament?

IN CASE HE GOT A HOLE-IN-ONE!

JUST JOKING!

What do you call a snowman in *Minecraft*'s desert biome?

A PUDDLE!

STAR POWER

Would you rather travel outer space with...?

☐ The Rescue Corps from *Pikmin* **OR** Samus Aran from *Metroid* ☐

Which would you rather be named after you, in a video game...?

☐ Constellation that looks like a donut **OR** Planet that looks like a meatball ☐

While travelling in space, would you rather visit...?

A planet from the *Mario Galaxy* games

OR

Popstar, the planet Kirby lives on

Rosalina lets you turn a Luma into a moon. Would you rather make...?

A moon that is a giant Rabbid head that talks

OR

A moon full of Star Bunnies

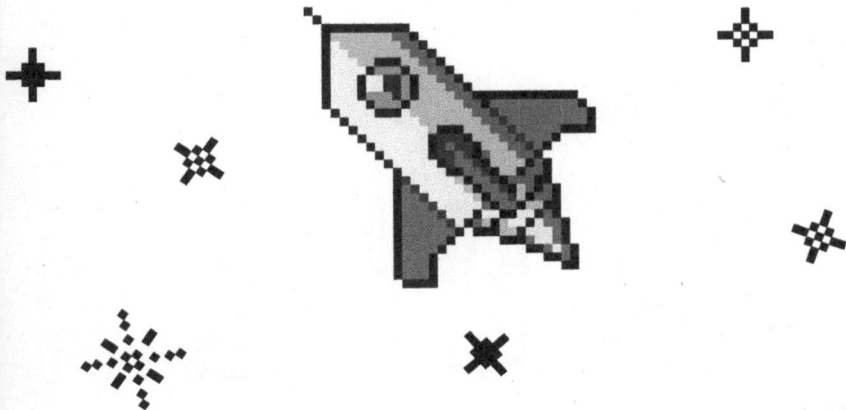

SERIOUS SPELLS

Would you rather cast magic like...?

Kamek and be able to teleport things and people

OR

Mallow from *Super Mario RPG* and be able to control the weather

What about a wand? Would you rather use...?

An *Animal Crossing* Magic Wand to change your clothes in a flash

OR

Kirby's Star Rod to shoot magic stars that sparkle and glow

If you could bring spells into a game that doesn't have them, would you add them to...?

☐ *Fall Guys* to mess up your opponents

OR

Animal Crossing to play pranks on the villagers ☐

What type of magic would you rather have in every game?

☐ The four elements: Air, Water, Earth, and Fire

OR

Magic that changes your character into another one ☐

HELPFUL INVENTIONS

Would you rather invent a machine that...?

☐ Pats your head when you finish a level

OR

Gives you a star sticker when you finish a level ☐

Would you rather invent a machine that...?

☐ Lets you eat and drink without taking your hands off your controller

OR

Can keep your hands at the perfect temperature ☐

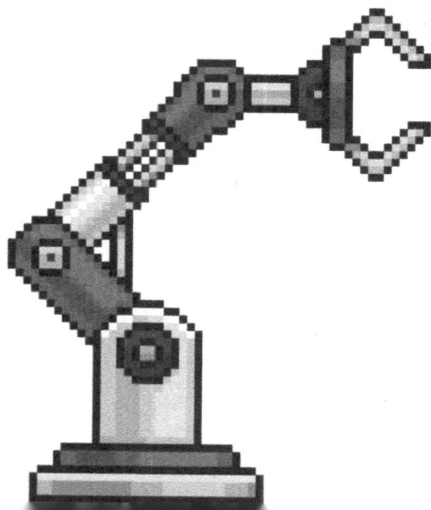

If a machine let you play video games in your sleep, would you...?

Use it to practise at a game you want to get better at

OR

Use it to play something dreamy to help you sleep better

If a machine let you play video games on any surface, would you...?

Play games on the walls of your room

OR

Play games on your desk at school

MUSICAL MOMENTS

**When school is about to end,
which music would you rather play?**

☐ The countdown music from the end of a *Splatoon* match

OR

'Hurry up' music from a *Mario* level ☐

**Which song would you rather play
whenever you hand in homework?**

☐ Music from finishing a *Sonic* level

OR

Music from finishing a *Kirby* level ☐

MUSICAL MOMENTS

Would you rather hear...?

☐ The *Mario Kart* Coconut Mall music play anytime you enter a room

OR

Minecraft music play anytime you are sitting down ☐

And would you rather hear...?

☐ *Super Mario* 'lose a life' music play whenever you fall down

OR

Kirby 'lose a life' music play whenever you bump into something ☐

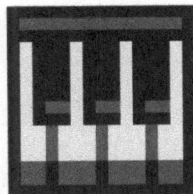

Which would you bring to stop boredom on a deserted island?

☐ A music player from *Animal Crossing* with every song loaded

OR

A completed Pokédex with info to read on every Pokémon ☐

Which *Breath of the Wild* outfit would you rather wear to a deserted island?

☐ The Zora Suit to let you swim easy and fast

OR

The Climbing Gear to let you climb anywhere ☐

When stranded, would you rather have...?

☐ *Animal Crossing* pockets full of fruits

OR

Mario & Luigi's suitcase full of mushrooms and honey ☐

Which *Undertale* character would you rather have with you on a deserted island?

☐ The bird that can slowly carry you over a gap

OR

Sans telling jokes but not helping much ☐

THE GREAT GAMING BAKE OFF

Whose recipe would you rather eat?

☐ Link's Monster Soup **OR** Alex's Suspicious Stew ☐

Which would you rather eat at a party?

☐ *Animal Crossing* cupcakes that look like your favourite villagers **OR** *Splatoon* cupcakes full of ink-coloured jam ☐

THE GREAT GAMING BAKE OFF

Would you rather make...?

☐ Strawberry shortcake with Princess Peach

OR

A Legendary Sweet Sandwich with Arven and Mabosstiff ☐

For your family, would you rather...?

☐ Cook a pasta dish with EXTRA garlic with Wario

OR

Bake giant banana bread with Diddy Kong ☐

BASE BUILDING

Would you rather live inside...?

☐ A secret base built into a *Minecraft* mountain

OR

A pokéball with the inside designed just for you ☐

If you could build a new playground at school, would you rather make one using...?

☐ Building parts from *LEGO Fortnite*

OR

Course parts from *Fall Guys* ☐

BASE BUILDING

Who would you rather share a home base with?

☐ Share a home base with the Koopalings and Bowser Jr.

OR

Share a home base with Donkey Kong and all of his Kong crew ☐

Which of these would you rather have...?

☐ A giant chest to store infinite extra items

OR

Helpful NPCs to do tasks for you when you're offline ☐

FANTASTIC FACTS

The Nintendo Company is over 130 years old. They used to make cards and toys before they started making videogames.

Sonic the Hedgehog was going to be a rabbit at first. He would have grabbed things with his ears. But the creators wanted a hero who could roll into a ball instead.

Why do Inklings collect so many clothes?

BECAUSE THEY'RE SHELLFISH!

JUST JOKING!

What Pokémon cheats at Hide-and-Seek?

PEAK-ACHU!

Which *Super Mario* Wonder power would you rather have?

A Drill Hat that never stops spinning

OR

A Bubble Cap that makes bubbles appear every time you speak

Which *Kirby* copy power would you rather have?

The Yo-Yo power to show off to the class

OR

The Microphone power to make everyone listen to you

LEVEL UP!

Would you rather use...?

A Mega Mushroom from **Super Mario**, but it only affects your head

OR

The Power Sneakers from **Sonic the Hedgehog**, but you can't stop until they run out!

What *Ratchet and Clank* item would you rather use on school bullies?

The Morph-O-Ray to turn them into chickens

OR

The Groovitron to force them to do silly dances

Who would make a better school caretaker?

Luigi with his special vacuum, the Poltergust

OR

Kirby with his special inhaling power

What kind of school would you rather go to?

A school in the world of *Splatoon*

OR

The academy in *Pokémon Scarlet and Violet*

TOO COOL FOR SCHOOL

Who would you rather have instead of a normal backpack?

☐ Banjo's grouchy bird partner, Kazooie **OR** Mario's robot water pack, FLUDD ☐

Who would you rather have as a teacher?

☐ Isabelle from *Animal Crossing* **OR** Goombella from *Paper Mario* ☐

**You get to direct a new movie!
Would you rather make...?**

☐ An action movie based on *Splatoon*

OR

A comedy movie based on *Mario + Rabbids* ☐

Which lesser-known *Sonic* hero would you rather see get a spin-off movie?

☐ Blaze the Cat with her fire magic

OR

Espio with his ninja skills ☐

TICKET

Something's missing... which movie would you rather have to watch?

☐ *Detective Pikachu* without Pikachu

OR

The *Super Mario Bros. Movie* without Mario ☐

Would you rather watch...?

☐ A new *Sonic* movie that's 100% animated like the *Mario* movie

OR

A new *Mario* movie that's live-action (in the real world) like the *Sonic* movie ☐

**Secret areas can be a hidden challenge!
Would you rather play...?**

A *Kirby* secret stage without being able to float or use powers

OR

A *Sonic* secret stage while only being able to see the very middle of the screen

Is it more exciting to find...?

A special cheat code that changes your character in a silly way

OR

A special level that's super hard but gives a useful reward

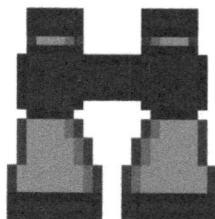

Would you rather discover a secret area in real life by...?

☐ Using a key on a magic keyhole hidden in a basement

OR

Going through a portal ring hidden inside a doghouse ☐

Wait a minute... something's not right here!
Would you rather be able to...?

☐ Glitch through walls randomly

OR

Touch objects to glitch them into other random things ☐

Which would you rather happen...?

☐ Your head sometimes glitched to be giant-sized

OR

Your arms sometimes glitched to be super long ☐

Would you rather have...?

Every *Mario* game ever but the enemy types glitch randomly

OR

Every *Sonic* game ever but sometimes the controls glitch to be reversed

Which of these would you rather play...?

Mario Kart but all the racers are invisible?

OR

Super Smash Bros. but the damage numbers are random?

TIMEY WIMEY

Where would you rather travel to?

☐ A time of knights and castles but you have Rivet's futuristic weapons

OR

A cyber future city but you have a Zelda's magic spells ☐

Would you rather travel with a herd of Yoshis across...?

☐ The Wild West **OR** Ancient China ☐

Would you rather wear Samus' mech suit to...?

☐ Hunt for pirate treasure **OR** Fight samurai and ninjas ☐

Which would be more fun to do while carried by a T-Rex?

☐ Race in *Mario Kart* tracks **OR** Run through *Sonic* levels ☐

**If you could see through time,
would you rather...?**

☐ See what the *Splatoon* world was like in the far past

OR

See what the *Pokémon* world will be like in the far future ☐

Which Paradox Pokémon would you rather partner with?

☐ Scream Tail, a mean-looking Jigglypuff from the past

OR

Iron Thorns, a robotic Tyranitar from the future ☐

Which would you rather have to fight?

☐ 10 primal Koopa Troopas with sharp teeth

OR

3 rocket-powered *Minecraft* Phantoms ☐

Who would you rather give you a tour of the ocean?

☐ Vaporeon  Kine the Fish ☐

Which of these areas would you rather explore an underwater version of?

☐ Moo Moo Farm, but instead of cows there are manatees  Green Hill Zone, but the grass is seaweed ☐

What's Yoshi's favourite Fortnite dance?

DINO-MITE BY BTS!

JUST JOKING!

Why did the cookie go to Dr. Mario?

BECAUSE IT FELT CRUMMY!

ON THE FARM

When playing a farming game,
would you rather have...?

☐ Crops that water themselves but you can't have any animals

OR

Animals that always love you but you can't plant any crops ☐

Which *Stardew Valley* item
would you pick in real life?

☐ A Warp Totem for your house

OR

A Glowstone Ring that gives off light ☐

Which animal would you rather get to pet at a real farm?

☐ Wooloo the round sheep Pokémon

OR

Chocobo the horse-like bird from *Final Fantasy* ☐

Where from a game would you rather build a farm in?

☐ The strange Boggly Woods from *Paper Mario*

OR

The cosy Natural Plains from *Kirby* ☐

Which would you rather protect your gaming farm from at night?

☐ *Pac-Man* Ghosts

OR

Skeletal Stalfos from *The Legend of Zelda* ☐

What would you rather grow on a farm in real life?

☐ Different berries from *Pokémon*

OR

Different blocky foods from *Minecraft* ☐

FANTASTIC FACTS

In Japan, *Super Mario Bros. 2* was a direct sequel to the first game with much harder levels. In other regions, Nintendo took a game called *Doki Doki Panic*, replaced the heroes with Mario characters, and called it *Super Mario Bros. 2.*

Kirby was first thought to be white, not pink, because the Game Boy system could not show colours. Later, when he was finally in a colour game, he got his pink colour.

DRESSING UP

Which *Fortnite* hero's outfits would you rather own for yourself?

☐ Jonesy **OR** Brite Bomber ☐

Would you rather have a shirt that...?

☐ Always shows your health bar **OR** Always shows what items you have ☐

Which would you rather wear to a disco?

☐ A purple Yoshi costume **OR** Princess Zelda's dress ☐

Which would you rather wear to school?

☐ Bowser's wedding outfit from *Mario Odyssey* **OR** A villager outfit from *Minecraft* ☐

CASTLES IN THE SAND

Which would you rather do on a beach?

☐ Take part in the Watermelon Festival on Gelato Beach (*Super Mario Sunshine*)

OR

☐ Search for pirate's gold in a shipwreck at Treasure Trove Cove (*Banjo-Kazooie*)

OR

☐ Dig for fossils on an *Animal Crossing* island beach

OR

☐ Have a Splattershot battle with an Inkling squad (*Splatoon*)

♥ ♥ ♥ ♡ ♡ ♡ ♡

Which would you rather do on a beach?

☐ Build sandcastles in the sand with the Toads on Peach Beach

OR

☐ Surf the waves with Alolan Raichu and Surfing Pikachu

OR

☐ Gather coconuts on the beach of Donkey Kong Island

OR

☐ Suck up tropical fruit with Kirby on the abandoned Everbay Coast

♡ ♡ ♡ ♡ ♥ ♥ ♥

Which would you rather drive in *Mario Kart*?

A really big kart you have to drive while standing

OR

A really tiny kart you can only fit your feet in

Which kind of screen would you rather have to play games on?

A screen that's the size of a postage stamp

OR

A screen the size of a whole football field

Which would you rather deal with?

☐ A tiny fly-sized Dr. Eggman buzzing your ear around all day

OR

A giant Snorlax always falling asleep in your path ☐

What kind of Yoshi would you keep at home?

☐ A really big, cuddly yarn Yoshi

OR

A litter of cute, sleepy baby Yoshis ☐

VS 100

Which Pokémon would you rather catch?

☐ 1 shiny Zygarde **OR** 100 regular Eevee ☐

Which Pokémon would you rather battle?

☐ 1 Level 100 Eternatus **OR** 100 Level 1 Smoliv ☐

GAME
OVER

Which would you rather find in a *Fortnite* match?

☐ 1 giant legendary Supply Llama  100 normal-sized Supply Llamas ☐

Who would you rather have on your side in a battle?

☐ 1 Donkey Kong  100 Shy Guys ☐

WINGS AND TAILS

Which Pokémon part would you rather add to a family pet?

☐ Zubat wings **OR** Vulpix tails ☐

Would you rather be able to fly with...?

☐ Pit's wings for 5 minutes a day **OR** Tails' two tails but for 10 seconds at a time ☐

What do you call a Yoshi that is sleeping?

A DINO-SNORE!

JUST JOKING!

What did the big piranha plant say to the little piranha plant?

"HEY, BUD!"

Would you rather have a picnic at...?

☐ Rosalina's Observatory, flying in space

OR

Atop a floating island in *Tears of the Kingdom* ☐

Would you rather have a BBQ...?

☐ With Koraidon on a tropical beach

OR

With Miraidon atop a mountain ☐

Which *Paper Mario* meal sounds tastier?

☐ Koopasta **OR** Mushroom Cake ☐

Which would you rather share with friends in real life?

☐ Potluck Soup from *Stardew Valley* **OR** A Mega Mountain Meal from *Splatoon* ☐

DRINK UP

Which odd drink are you grabbing to power up?

☐ A jar of Slurp Juice from *Fortnite*

OR

Crab-N-Go bagged drinks from *Splatoon* ☐

Which would you rather try?

☐ Bloxy Cola from *Roblox*

OR

Joja Cola from *Stardew Valley* ☐

Which powered-up sweet thing would you rather eat?

☐ Invincible Candy from *Kirby*   **OR**   Electro Pop from *Paper Mario* ☐

If you could spend a day in *Kirby's Dream Buffet*, would you rather...?

☐ Learn how to roll and race to win the most strawberries   **OR**   Take your time eating every kind of treat in sight ☐

FACE PAINT

Would you rather wear face paint that...?

☐ Looks like a Boo and makes you invisible when you cover your face

OR

Looks like a Jigglypuff and lets you sing any song you want ☐

If you could paint buttons on your face that actually work, would you...?

☐ Paint your nose to be the power button on your game consoles?

OR

Paint your cheeks to be the volume buttons? ☐

How does Lara Croft start a letter?

"TOMB IT MAY CONCERN..."

JUST JOKING!

Knock Knock, who's there?

BOO.

Boo who?

NO NEED TO CRY! IT'S A FRIENDLY BOO!

DANCE OFF

Would you rather...?

☐ Be able to do any *Fortnite* dance once a day

OR

Make someone else do the default *Fortnite* dance once a day ☐

Would you rather...?

☐ Dance like a robot with the Squid Sisters

OR

Do disco moves with Pearl and Marina ☐

Would you rather dance to...?

☐ Pop music with Amy Rose **OR** Heavy metal with Waluigi ☐

Whenever you dance, would you rather...?

☐ Be able to copy yourself like Kirby **OR** Be able to make your own victory theme play ☐

BETTER TOGETHER

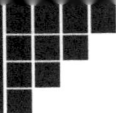

Who would you rather have play as Goouigi to help you in *Luigi's Mansion*?

☐ Your next-door neighbour   **OR**   Your teacher ☐

Would you rather play *Kirby* co-op with...?

☐ Everyone sharing lives and a life bar   **OR**   Everyone always has to use the same copy power ☐

LEVEL UP!

Would you rather play *Overcooked*...?

☐ Without anyone being allowed to speak

OR

With everyone holding their controllers upside-down ☐

Would you rather play *Moving Out* where...?

☐ Players can't see their screen, someone tells them what to do

OR

Players are only able to use one hand and one foot to play ☐

PRINCESS POWER

Which Princess would you rather have become headmistress of your school?

☐ Princess Zelda **OR** Princess Peach ☐

Which Princess would you rather play sports with?

☐ Princess Daisy **OR** Blaze the Cat ☐

Would you rather become royalty of...?

☐ The Kingdom of Hyrule **OR** The Mushroom Kingdom ☐

Would you rather rule a kingdom where...?

☐ Magic is real, but everyone shares one mana bar **OR** Power ups are real but must always be shared ☐

Would you rather be able to make the real world look like...?

☐ The blocky world of *Minecraft* **OR** The pixel world of *Stardew Valley* ☐

Would you rather be able to change the world's...?

☐ Volume setting **OR** Colour setting ☐

Which creatures would you rather have become real?

☐ 50 random Pokémon

OR

All of the *Animal Crossing* villagers ☐

Would you rather live in a world where...?

☐ Everyone drives in *Mario Kart* machines?

OR

Everyone can carry 10 items at a time ☐

MONSTER MASH-UP

Which would you rather have on your basketball team?

☐ A Goomba with Donkey Kong's arms **OR** A Koopa Troopa with Sonic's legs ☐

Which would you rather have help with chores?

☐ A Wiggler with all hands instead of feet **OR** A Minecraft Zombie with Kirby head ☐

MONSTER MASH-UP

Which would be more fun to play football with?

☐ Motobugs from *Sonic* that have Spiny shells

OR

Octarians from *Splatoon* that have racoon tails ☐

Which would you rather be for a day?

☐ A Chain Chomp with a Yoshi tongue

OR

An Awoofy with Piranha Plant teeth ☐

This is it, hero! An army of evil minions stands in your way to the final big bad boss lair. How will you fight?

☐ Charge into battle on Epona, wielding an enchanted diamond sword

OR

Distract the minions with a Mario Kart tournament while Tails and Knuckles help you to fly over ☐

You made it to the boss door, but it isn't opening...

☐ Use Zelda's magic to find a key

OR

Ask Mewtwo to help you open the door by force ☐

It's the final boss... the writer of this book! I've used all your answers to plot the perfect defence. Bwahahahaaaa!

Wait- no! What are you doing!?

Get the Mario Bros. to rain down fireballs that turn Sonic into a furry ball of flame

OR

Get Kirby to use copy powers while *Splatoon* agents use all their Special Weapons

Drats! You've defeated me.
Oh, go on... I guess you've earned a celebration.

Throw a big disco party in Hyrule Castle with tons of food

OR

Play *Mario Party* with your friends on a giant cake as big as a playground

Congratulations. You made it all the way to the end!
Need help knowing who's who? Here's a list of the
videogame names you might have seen in this book,
and a game series you can find them in!

Alex - Minecraft
Alolan Raichu - Pokémon
Amy Rose - Sonic the Hedgehog
Arven - Pokémon
Awoofy - Kirby
Banjo - Banjo-Kazooie
Beep-0 - Mario + Rabbids
Big Man - Splatoon
Big Yeetus - Fall Guys
Blastoise - Pokémon
Blaze the Cat - Sonic the Hedgehog
Blooper - Super Mario
Boo - Super Mario
Bowser - Super Mario
Bowser Jr. - Super Mario
Brite Bomber - Fortnite
Captain Toad - Super Mario
Chain Chomp - Super Mario
Charizard - Pokémon
Chao - Sonic the Hedgehog
Chell - Portal
Clanker - Banjo-Kazooie
Coco - Crash Bandicoot
Creeper - Minecraft
Crash - Crash Bandicoot
Daisy - Super Mario
Dedede - Kirby
Diddy Kong - Super Mario
DJ Octavio - Splatoon
Donkey Kong - Super Mario
Eevee - Pokémon

Eggman (aka Robotnik) - Sonic
Enderman - Minecraft
Ender Dragon - Minecraft
Epona - Legend of Zelda
Espio - Sonic the Hedgehog
Eternatus - Pokémon
Finizen - Pokémon
Flowey - Undertale
FLUDD - Super Mario
Ganon - Legend of Zelda
Gengar - Pokémon
GlaDOS - Portal
Goomba - Super Mario
Goombella - Paper Mario
Gyroid - Animal Crossing
Isabelle - Animal Crossing
Iron Thorns - Pokémon
Jigglypuff - Pokémon
Jonesy - Fortnite
Kamek - Super Mario
Kazooie - Banjo-Kazooie
Kine - Kirby
Kirby - Kirby
KK Slider - Animal Crossing
Koopa Troopa - Super Mario
Koopalings - Super Mario
Knuckles - Sonic the Hedgehog
Koraidon - Pokémon
Lapras - Pokémon
Link - Legend of Zelda
Luigi - Super Mario

Loftwing - Legend of Zelda
Mabosstiff - Pokémon
Magikarp - Pokémon
Mallow - Super Mario RPG
Marina - Splatoon
Mario - Super Mario
Meowscles - Fortnite
Meta-Knight - Kirby
Mewtwo - Pokémon
Miraidon - Pokémon
Moblin - Legend of Zelda
Motobug - Sonic
Mudsdale - Pokémon
Nemona - Pokémon
Neo Cortex - Crash Bandicoot
Octarians - Splatoon
Pac-Man - Pac-Man
Papyrus - Undertale
Peach - Super Mario
Pearl - Splatoon
Penny - Pokémon
Peely - Fortnite
Piranha Plant - Super Mario
Phantom - Minecraft
Pikachu - Pokémon
Pit - Kid Icarus
Rabbid - Mario + Rabbids
Rabbid Peach - Mario + Rabbids
Rapidash - Pokémon
Ratchet - Ratchet and Clank
Redstone Golem - Minecraft
Rito - Legend of Zelda
Rivet - Ratchet and Clank
ROB the Robot - Nintendo (toy)
Robotnik (aka Eggman) - Sonic
Rosalina - Super Mario
Rouge the Bat - Sonic the Hedgehog

Samus Aran - Metroid
Sans - Undertale
Satori - Legend of Zelda
Scream Tail - Pokémon
Shadow - Sonic the Hedgehog
Sheik - Legend of Zelda
Shy Guy - Super Mario
Sirfetch'd - Pokémon
Smoliv - Pokémon
Snorlax - Pokémon
Sonic - Sonic the Hedgehog
Spiny - Super Mario
Stalhorse - Legend of Zelda
Star Bunny - Super Mario Galaxy
Steve - Minecraft
Squid Sisters (Callie and Marie) - Splatoon
Supply Llama - Fortnite
Tails (aka Miles) - Sonic the Hedgehog
Tallneck - Horizon
Tawna - Crash Bandicoot
Team Rocket - Pokémon
Timmy & Tommy - Animal Crossing
Toad - Super Mario
Tom Nook - Animal Crossing
Vaporeon - Pokémon
Vulpix - Pokémon
Waddle Dee - Kirby
Wario - Super Mario
Waluigi - Super Mario
Wiggler - Super Mario
Yoshi - Super Mario
Zelda - Legend of Zelda
Zora - Legend of Zelda
Zubat - Pokémon

GAME OVER